The Agile Manager's Guide To

GETTING
ORGANIZED

The Agile Manager's Guide To

GETTING ORGANIZED

By Jeff Olson

Velocity Business Publishing
Bristol, Vermont USA

For Christina

Copyright © 1997, 2001 by Velocity Business Publishing, Inc.

All Rights Reserved

Library of Congress Catalog Card Number 97-90830

ISBN 0-9659193-0-7

Title page illustration by Elayne Sears

Second printing, June 1999

Third printing, October 2001

Printed in Canada

If you'd like additional copies of this book or a catalog of books in the Agile Manager Series®, please get in touch.

- **Write us:**
  Velocity Business Publishing, Inc.
  15 Main Street
  Bristol, VT 05443 USA

- **Call us:**
  1-888-805-8600 in North America (toll-free)
  1-802-453-6669 from all other countries

- **Fax us:**
  1-802-453-2164

- **E-mail us:**
  action@agilemanager.com

- **Visit our Web site:**
  www.agilemanager.com

The Web site contains much of interest to business people—tips, downloads, courses, and more.

Contents

Books in the Agile Manager Series®:

Introduction

Don't buy this book because you want to get more things done. Buy it because you want to get the right things done. The things that, completed, will make you feel fulfilled, productive, and happy.

Because the purpose of getting organized is to get results, on the job or at home. It's not about increasing your ability to cram more into your life. You're busy enough already.

And getting organized is about more than just managing time. It's about identifying the things that matter to you and then organizing your life so you attend to them. Whether it's a big project at work, your kids, volunteer activities, or getting that promotion.

Further, if you want to spend less time at work, you came to the right place. As management consultant and philosopher Richard Moran once wrote, "The person who spends all of his or her time at work is not hard-working; he or she is boring."

The most important thing at work, of course, is to get results. You can do that with a lot of effort, or with a little effort applied in key spots. Most of this book is devoted to helping you reduce the effort required to get results at work. With the extra time in your life, you can get back to the things, like music, cooking, collecting, or sports, that make you a well-rounded (i.e., non-boring) person. And a better manager.

This book will help you excel at work without neglecting the non-work people and hobbies that make life worth living. First you'll identify the important things in your life. Then you'll get a few tools and techniques to ensure you spend your time effectively—on the things that make a big difference to you and others around you.

You can read *Getting Organized* in one or two sittings at the most, then refer to it again and again as you need to. The contents and the index, and the "Best Tips" and "Agile Manager's Checklist" boxes, make it easy to find what you're looking for.

In short, *The Agile Manager's Guide to Getting Organized* will help you get maximum results with the least amount of effort.

The Fundamentals
Of Getting Organized

*"But at my back I always hear
Time's winged chariot hurrying near."*

— ANDREW MARVELL IN
"TO HIS COY MISTRESS"

Chapter One

Banish Mental Clutter

The Agile Manager looked down at the list on the bottom of his clipboard. His three career goals. He looked at the list frequently; he wanted to feel, always, that he was on track. He had left more than one "dream" job, to the amazement of many, because they threatened to carry him away from his goals.

He pondered the middle goal. It said, "Don't go to stupid business functions at the expense of spending time with family." Well, he thought, it's clear. I won't go to the company Christmas party this year. I won't miss Janey's school pageant. But it'll blow Don's top. He'll take it as an affront. Oh, well. I'll get along—I think.

Clutter slows you down. And it's not just the paper you can't find or the file box you trip over or the trouble you have deciding what to do next. It's the mental clutter that precedes these mishaps.

The clutter in your life takes many forms—from too much paper to things misplaced to too much to do. And it's all a symptom of deeper reasons. It might be the inability to make a decision. It might be the desire to be liked by all that gives rise to the inability to say "no." It could be the great joy some get in

11

building mental castles that somehow never get built in the real world. (While real pieces of the dreams lay all over the place.)

Clutter is also a function of a common myth: You'll have more time later. "Later," however, is always worse. You've left so many things undone that the time crunch seems to deepen and become even more overwhelming.

Know the Culprit Behind Clutter

Before you can get out from under clutter, you must identify what you want to do with your life. You must create goals.

Create goals? What does that have to do with clutter? Everything. Many people afflicted by clutter have no grand plans. They live day-to-day and believe life is something to get through, not take control of.

> **Best Tip**
>
> Create goals. It's the only way you can identify what is important to you—and make good decisions.

As a result, everything that happens is of the same importance, and decisions are hard to make: "Jim wants me to work on this project first, but Sandy wants me to work on that one. Which should I do?" Or, "Should I give to this charity or that one? Should I go to the ballet next Thursday with Beth or to the ball game with Bill? Should I take a pottery class or something on marketing? Should I throw out information about this organization? If I do, should I throw information about that one away? But maybe I'll want to join both some time . . ."

The solution to avoiding such questions in the first place is simple. You need a system that can help you identify what is important to you. That system is not hard to construct.

Identify Your Goals and Objectives in Life

You no doubt bought this book to get more organized at work. Understand, then, that the step you're about to take is of vital importance in getting organized and achieving results in any area of life, but especially at work. Study after study has shown that those who set goals for themselves achieve the most in life— the most money and material goods, and the greatest fulfillment and inner peace.

Take out a piece of paper or sit at the computer and write down your goals in life. Come up with one explicit, key goal (or at most two) for each of these areas:

- Family/friends
- Work/professional
- Community/volunteer
- Education/intellectual
- Hobby
- Leisure/travel
- Sports
- Spiritual
- Financial

Here are some sample goals:

Family/friends: I will stay in touch with my friends by writing at least one letter a week.

Work/professional: I will make vice president within three years.

Community/volunteer: I will help out at the local soup kitchen once a month.

Education/intellectual: I will get certified to teach school by 2001.

Hobby: I will make a dining room table in 2004.

Leisure/travel: I will take a two-week vacation to Sonoma County, California, this year.

Sports: I will break 80 in golf by 2008.

Spiritual: I will find a church compatible with my beliefs and attend services at least twice a month.

Financial: I will retire with at least $1 million in assets by age sixty-five.

Make Goals Specific and Measurable

The goals just listed are specific and they are measurable. Such specificity leads to fulfillment in the areas you deem important. They can help you define the purposes in your life and thereby organize it most efficiently. Most important, they can help you decide among the dozens of alternative actions you face each week if not each day.

Best Tip
Identify and pursue just one or two goals in each area of your life. Any more than that and you'll soon have a daunting list that will depress you rather than add energy to your life.

For example, if you're going to break 80 in golf, you know you have to spend time playing and practicing. If the choice is to go out and chip a hundred balls or watch television, you'll know what to do.

Similarly, if you're going to make VP in three years, you won't have any trouble deciding how to use your time: lunching with the right people, maneuvering at work to get assigned the right projects, perhaps getting an MBA at night, and so on.

Attaching dates to your goals keeps you on track. Did you get that certification in 2001? Why not? What must you do now to get it?

Goals: Your Values in Action

Are the goals you wrote down the right things to do? Of course. They embody your values. For example, if one of your goals is "I will spend whatever it takes to put my children through college," you are showing how much you value both your children and education.

Some goals, especially in the career and financial areas, may need to be tempered with a good dose of ethics. You don't want to give yourself license to lie, cheat, and steal just to get that beach house in Bermuda, for example.

Pay particular attention to your career goals. They are the benchmarks or values you will use at work to make all kinds of decisions.

The work-and-career category is one where you may want more than a few goals. You might have some that concern your earnings, ultimate position of authority, owning your own business one day, and what you will and will not do to achieve your ultimate aims (like sacrifice your family, or undermine the work of others).

Stretch!

If the goals you come up with aren't too challenging, try again, at least in a few areas. It's only by stretching, by getting out of our comfort zones, that we grow and learn to handle more of what life throws at us. And it's only by stretching that we achieve the truly worthwhile in life.

Be Flexible

Review your goals frequently and don't have too many.

I once made a list of thirty-five goals. Because I'd made progress in only a few areas, my list depressed me eventually. I ended up burying it in a file cabinet.

Now I have six key goals. Rather than depressing me, glancing at the list energizes me.

Further, don't be afraid to change your goals. As you and your values change, so should your goals. They should encourage you to excel, not handcuff you. Review them yearly, at least, to ensure they still fit.

If you're having trouble coming up with energizing goals, it may help to read a book like Stephen Covey's *First Things First*, or Richard Bolles's classic *What Color Is Your Parachute?* These two authors can help you sort out what's really important to you.

Deciding what you want out of all areas of life is your first giant step toward getting organized. The next is identifying how you can best contribute at work.

Focus on Your Contribution at Work

If you're reading this book, succeeding at work is important to you.

Yet work is the place where poor habits of organization are deadliest. Word gets around if you procrastinate and can't meet deadlines. People look at you funny when you can't find important reports or memos. It's painfully obvious to all when you go into a meeting unprepared. And most sinful in the eyes of superiors is working hard on inconsequential matters.

There's a simple way to know what to do and when to do it. As Peter Drucker points out in his classic *The Effective Executive*, "Knowledge work is not defined by quantity. Neither is it defined by its costs. Knowledge work is defined by its results."

To succeed at work, then, you must know what results are expected of you. If you don't know, ask. Sometimes you're lucky enough to set your own standards for results. But even then you still have to perform by turning those results into sales or profit increases, money saved, or market share gained.

Focusing on results, of course, focuses you. That reduces clutter, mental or physical, to a minimum. You'll work faster.

Effective work, incidentally, isn't busy or frenzied. As Drucker points out, well-organized managers doing important work may look dull and plodding. That's because they have had the foresight to anticipate problems and eliminate or avoid them. Contrast such dull-but-effective workers with rough-riding, crisis-loving, cowboy managers who equate a high stress level with getting things done.

Know Your Prime Tasks

Most of you will know what your most important tasks are. They are what you were hired for. And they are things that usually can't be delegated. They are the areas of contribution in which you personally affect the company's health for better or worse.

To succeed at work—and organize your time to do so—you must know what your superiors' expectations are. If you're at all fuzzy about what you should be contributing, then it's possible your superiors are a little fuzzy. Have them clarify your job for the benefit of all.

If you're the one setting priorities for your company or work group or self, remember Drucker's cardinal rule for business success: Feed the opportunities and starve the problems. Never try to shore up failing or mature businesses or product lines by wasting good people on them.

Knowing how you can contribute at work is your fundamental organizing principle: You know the few key areas in which your results will be judged. There's no doubt as to what's important, and thus what you should give your attention to.

Unfortunately, even when you know what's important, it is not always easy to get to it. Organizational life means one thing: interruptions. The tools and techniques in Section Two will help you deal with that aspect. So will the last of the fundamental concepts, and the subject of our next chapter: simplify your life.

The Agile Manager's Checklist

✔ To reduce clutter, create goals.

✔ Do it now. You won't have more time later.

✔ Create just a handful of goals in each important area of your life.

✔ Get organized at work. Poor organizational skills are deadly to your career.

✔ At work, use career goals as benchmarks to make decisions.

✔ Set challenging goals. Stretch!

✔ Focus on one thing at work: results.

✔ Identify the most important thing you can do at work to influence the company positively. Then do it.

Chapter Two

Simplify, Simplify

It was Tom from sales. "We need you down in the conference room right away to explain the Fuller situation." The Agile Manager swung the phone cord in loops as he figured out what to do. Think fast, he said to himself.

"Sorry, I can't do it right now, Tom. I'm in the middle of something." Tom sputtered. The power situation was a bit ambiguous, but Tom clearly believed the Agile Manager would hop out of his chair and sprint to the conference room. Hope I'm not misjudging this one, thought the Agile Manager.

"But we need you here now," said Tom. "You're the only one who knows all the facts about what happened with the order." A pleading tone had entered his voice. Score!

"I'm sorry. I'd be happy to schedule something even as early as this afternoon. But I can't right now." Which was true. The Agile Manager was completely focused on a spreadsheet that analyzed the cost basis for a key part in a new product. To leave it now would mean having to rebuild the road his thoughts had created in the past ninety minutes.

"Thanks a lot," Tom snorted as he slammed the telephone down. The Agile Manager shrugged him off and was soon back inside *the spreadsheet. He'd make it up within the next week by feeding Tom some choice piece of information about the new product effort.*

A key aspect of getting organized is to simplify your life. You went a long way toward doing that in the last chapter by identifying what is important to you. Doing so allows you to reject or keep at arm's length the unimportant. "Will I join the school board? Gee, I'm sorry but I already have a couple of volunteer positions, and I can't handle any more. Thanks for thinking of me, though!"

Part one of leading a simpler life, then, is cutting down on the sheer number of activities you get involved in. Don't worry if you feel you've cut out too much. You can always add things back, especially if you realize some activities were more important to you than you thought.

Part two of simplicity is, well, simple: one thing at a time. My father-in-law once remarked, upon seeing a boy driving a car and trying to kiss a girl at the same time, "He's doing two important things badly."

Same goes for you any time you try to juggle tasks without giving full attention to either. Or when you're trying to concentrate on something important for a few hours but keep getting interrupted. Sometimes that means pushing away co-workers who want your time when *they* need it. But people will take advantage of you if they know you're always available at their whim. Don't encourage their poor planning by giving in—unless, of course, a direct superior wants something.

A good way to do one thing at a time? Clear your desk of everything but the task at hand. One task. Then tackle it until it's finished.

An important technique in getting things done, to be discussed later, is to get many tasks in motion at the same time. But that doesn't mean juggling them, or flitting from one to the next as the mood strikes you.

First Things First

Barry Eigen, former head of a medical-supply firm in Milwaukee called HealthCall, wrote a book (*How to Think Like a Boss*) on what the achievers in his company did to get ahead. Most had a special talent for knowing precisely, on a daily basis, what they could do to contribute to the firm. And then doing it first. Not after drinking a cup of coffee and reading a trade magazine. Not after setting up lunch dates and tennis matches. Not after attending to easy things on their to-do lists.

If all you ever did was concentrate on the most important tasks, and forgot about all the rest, you'd never lose a job. You'd be far too valuable.

You know, or should know, your priorities at work. Make sure they land at the top of your to-do list.

Aim to Contribute

Use this chart to assess what you should be working on and to highlight the time-wasters. As an exercise, enlarge it on a copier. Take your to-do list and put each item somewhere on it. (If you don't have one handy, just fill in the day's activities.)

Doing this exercise every so often will help keep you focused. If it proves useful, you may want to use it in conjunction with a to-do list—or *as* a to-do list.

CONTRIBUTION CHART			
Contribution	Cannot Wait	Can Wait	Time-waster

Let's look at what occupies each column:

Contribution: These are the activities you've identified as critical to the success of your organization (or whatever major projects you're working on in any area of life). They may include hiring someone for a key position, selling, training a new employee, working on a special project, planning for the near future, thinking up new products, revamping processes or procedures, or grinding out the work you were hired to do.

Cannot wait: Items in this column include such things as the task the boss just handed you with a tight deadline, everyday problems that demand attention, or a crisis.

Can wait: This column is for things you need to get around to, but which aren't pressing. They may include cleaning out your files, filling out paperwork, or staying in touch with colleagues. Find time to attend to them, or they'll turn into a logjam.

This column can also include important items—like getting ready for a speech or planning for next year—but shift them into the "Contribution" column as deadlines approach.

Time-waster: Things you should push away from you, fast: inconsequential work you could avoid, dealing with much of your e-mail and many of your phone calls, drop-in visitors, and things like television, complaining, or playing games at your computer.

The more you stay in the "Contribution" column, the farther you'll go in your career.

Take Care of Today, Not Tomorrow

"I recommend to you to take care of the minutes; for the hours will take care of themselves," said Lord Chesterfield a few centuries ago. He may as well have added, "the months and the years will also take care of themselves."

Once you have your priorities set, even if they are big and important ones, get down to work. You know the cliché—"Every journey of a thousand miles begins with a few small steps."

Dreaming of a rosy future holds two perils: First, you're never going to reach it if all you do is dream. To live in your dream house, you have to pick up a hammer at some point.

Second, the future is unknown. You might escape into comforting dreams because you believe life may not turn out as you plan. Disaster may strike. You may get fired. Your business may fail. Your friends may turn on you . . . and on and on. You think about all the bad things that might ruin your plans. As a result, you lose enthusiasm for what you're doing. Or you're scared out of doing anything at all.

The only antidote to such poisonous thoughts is to get busy with today and forget about tomorrow.

The Beauty of 'No'

The last of the fundamentals of getting organized is to learn to say "no." No, I can't join the group. No, I can't help out this week. No, I don't want to join that task force. No, I can't drive you to the airport tomorrow.

Say no to the things and people that aren't important to you. Having to add tasks and activities to your day at the behest of others complicates your life enormously, especially if they are long-term. Suddenly you've lost control of what you want to do and are doing what others want done—to make *their* lives easier.

You don't need to become a "no" monster. If it's an old friend, of course you'll take her to the airport. If the school is becoming decrepit, of course you'll join the board and help rebuild it. If it would be a good move for your career, then you'd be happy to join the task force on compensation.

But bear in mind, always, what's important to *you*.

The Agile Manager's Checklist

✔ Stick to one important task at a time.
✔ Take care of today's work. Worry about tomorrow in twenty-four hours or so.
✔ Learn to say "no."

Organize to Save Time

"Time and I against any two."

—SPANISH PROVERB

Chapter Three

Three Basic Tools For Getting Organized

The Agile Manager had to create a timeline for Project Simmer. Simmer was an enhancement to one of the company's core products that would let it enter the Asian market. Enter? Astonish is more like it, he thought to himself.

But the timeline would take at least four uninterrupted hours. Where to find that amid the knocks on his office door, the ringing telephone, the fifty-three e-mail messages in his in-box, and the dopes down the hall who wanted to talk hockey? Only one thing to do, he thought.

"Steve?"

"Yeah?" answered his assistant.

"Tomorrow morning I'll be consulting with an important person until at least 11:30. Cover for me."

"Okay, boss."

The next day the Agile Manager walked in at 11:15 A.M., timeline in hand.

"How's that important person?" Steve asked with a grin.

"Couldn't be better," said the Agile Manager, giving Steve a quick wink while striding toward his office door. And why not? He not only finished the timeline working at home, but he enjoyed

breakfast with his daughter and got her on the school bus without a hitch.

The phone buzzed. The boss. "I've been thinking that the deadline I gave you to come up with the timeline was too short. I know you have a lot on your plate. So Thursday would be fine instead of tomorrow."

"It's all done. I'll bring it in to you right away." He winked again at Steve as he whistled down the hall.

Planning to accomplish the important things in your life requires but three tools. And the first of them you can probably dispense with after a day or two. The tools are:

1. **A time log.**
2. **A to-do list.**
3. **A desk or pocket calendar with enough space to hold appointments.**

How much you spend for these items is up to you. You can spend as little as nothing by doing it all on scrap paper and using one of the small calendars you probably get as a holiday gift at work, or you can spend hundreds of dollars on fancy, leatherbound planners. But just remember: Expensive planners won't help you plan your day more efficiently.

Where Does Your Time Go?

The first thing to do to gain control of your life is to discover where your time goes. If you want some fun, sit down now and guess where it goes, hour by hour, throughout the day. Your mind will tell you quite briskly that you spend a goodly amount of time prospecting, or coaching new hires, planning, staying in touch with key customers, or whatever else your key duties are.

Your time log will tell you otherwise.

It will tell you, for instance, just how much time you spend discussing the market with your broker, or last night's football game with the guys around the water cooler. It will tell you how much time that nonsensical phone call from a superior wasted. It will tell you how many items, most of them both pressing and unimportant, stood between you and that one truly important call to a vendor to discuss a problem.

Keeping a log is simple. Keep a small notebook or piece of paper near you at all times. Note how you use your time from minute to minute. For example:

Best Tip
For just one day, figure out where your time goes minute by minute, hour by hour.

9:15 Call from husband about dog
9:18 José popped in unannounced to discuss marketing plan
9:39 Used bathroom
9:44 Started memo on expanding into Utah
9:47 Call from headhunter
9:48 Back to memo
9:52 Boss needs figures on Murphy plan
10:12 Back to memo
10:31 Finished memo; check e-mail
10:36 Call from Jim on the road; needs documents faxed
10:49 Back to e-mail
11:01 Finished e-mail; sort regular mail
11:08 Connie calls about dinner date
11:14 Look at mail and skim trade magazines
11:45 Lunch with Hector

And so on. This process will be excruciating at first, but stick with it. It's important. You'll find how many interruptions you get, how many of them could probably be avoided, and how little time you have to work on the important things—the areas in which you can contribute.

You'll see that it wasn't necessary to take Connie's call, especially once she started talking about a new boyfriend; that José's twenty minutes on the marketing plan could have taken ten—and it would have been better if he'd buzzed you first and set up a time to do so; that Jim, notoriously disorganized, called you to fax documents because he knew you'd be there and that you'd do it (but you could have delegated the job to someone else); that you spent more time than you should have looking at your mail because you didn't want to start something more important just before lunch, etc.

Keep a log for a day or week—however long it takes you to realize that if you're to get organized and contribute in meaningful ways, you have to gain some control over your day. And that means finding blocks of time in which you can work undisturbed.

How to Plan Your Day

Now that you know how little time you spend on the things that really need doing—all of which conspire to keep you disorganized and working late to meet deadlines—take five minutes every morning to plot your day and week. Even better, do it the night before.

The to-do list. Most people keep a to-do list in some form. If you don't, start. You can't plan your day without one.

I suggest a two-part to-do list. On the top, keep a list of the mundane things you have to do or schedule. Examples:

1. *Make car appt.*
2. *Clean up Henderson files*
3. *Call lawyer about will*
4. *Send in estimated taxes*

Write down such things throughout the day as you think of them.

On the bottom, keep a list of the long-term important things. These may be a mixture of work- and home-related items:

- *Begin outline for speech at trade show*
- *Think of name for product*
- *Reengineer order processing (Nov. deadline)*

- *Hire for Stan's old job*
- *Take seminar on budgeting*
- *Get to Roberta's soccer games twice a month*

Usually these are things that can't be done all at once or that recur.

If you're not sure where something fits, look back at the contribution chart in the last chapter for help categorizing it.

Consult your calendar. Now block out time on the calendar to take care of your "to-do" items. You may have to build your day around appointments with others or meetings. Put those down first. Then make appointments with yourself. Make long appointments to get the long-term important things done. Schedule one or more short periods to do things like open the mail or return phone calls.

Best Tip

If you can, work at home two mornings a week. If you can't, find a room at the office to hide out in.

Leave the rest of the time free for the inevitable unplanned events, both important and not important, that will intrude.

Lump similar tasks together whenever you can. Read all your e-mail once a day for fifteen minutes, for example. Return phone calls twice a day—once late in the morning, once late in the afternoon.

Don't try to plan more than 60-70 percent of your day. It probably won't turn out the way you imagine. Leaving a third of the day free recognizes organizational realities—that you will face a crisis, socialize a bit, put out a fire or two, or suddenly have to write a five-page fact sheet the boss wants on his desk by noon.

Overplanning is a sure way to get depressed. If you fill your day, you'll never get as much done as you'd hoped and it will end up stressing you out.

Avoid interruptions. The important thing about the long appointments you schedule with yourself is that no one interrupt. Try closing your door. Let your secretary or voice mail system take all phone calls. Hide in an unused room. Stay home or go to a neutral site to do your work.

If people balk, especially superiors, let them know how productive you are during these periods. Of course, you can always allow phone calls from a select few.

How much uninterrupted time should you take? Depends on your position. Low- to mid-level managers can usually get away with more than senior executives. Peter Drucker estimates that senior executives can usually control only a quarter of their time.

Best Tip

Make appointments with yourself, and don't let anyone interrupt them.

Where to find time. If you really, really can't keep people away from you for long periods of time, then get up early in the morning to work at home and come into the office as late as you can without arousing uncharitable thoughts in others. Or come in two hours before everyone else.

That's far preferable to doing work at home each evening or on the weekend—save that time to spend with your family, attend to personal matters, and recharge your batteries.

If you're disciplined, you can find a fair amount of such quality time while traveling. On a long flight, for instance. (By the way, need to silence a talkative seatmate? Tell him you're with the IRS.) Or cluster your appointments in a distant city so you can spend a morning or afternoon working in your hotel room.

Use a Planner?

If you can do all your time planning on inexpensive paper, why buy a fancy planner? Some people like them. Some people respond well to the rigor a planner imposes, or the philosophy of time management that stands behind it.

I used an expensive planner for a few years, and it did a great job sharpening my sense of what I wanted out of life, what the priority items were on a daily basis, and how I spent my day. Once that happened, though, I decided I didn't need to spend money each year on new pages, binders for the old ones, and so on. I also found that my notes for each day, while important for a week or a month, had little lasting importance.

Your situation may be different. A planner may motivate you. Or, if you're a lawyer or other professional, you may need a handy way to keep pages of notes for years.

Try one out. It won't hurt. It'll even feel good to begin with. Like you're on top of things. But as in all matters, you'll only get out of it what you put into it.

Computer Programs: Getting Better

You see more and more people using their computers as planning systems. Microsoft Outlook, for example, is a good program that does all the things you need it to do—remember appointments, track projects, keep to-do lists, hold a database of contacts, and more. If you have a sound card and speakers, the program will remind you ahead of time of upcoming appointments.

A program like that works fine for those chained to computers, but what about people who travel around during the day, or those with a variety of work and non-work activities? You might consider buying one of the Palm OS-powered handheld devices made by Palm, Handspring, Sony, and others. You can do all the things we've discussed here—create a time log, keep to-do lists, move things onto a calendar, set alarms, and a lot more.

Best of all, they are portable. The main danger is that you'll reach for your Palm or Visor one day and discover it's not there. You'll probably find it at home—under the pillow of your daughter, who snatched it to play Sub Hunt in the dark the night before.

Deadlines: A Motivating Secret of Achievers

Here's a secret the agile managers among you know very well: You can seem like Superman by giving yourself pretty stiff deadlines to get important things done. And then moving them up.

Giving yourself deadlines and adhering to them as though the Almighty set them does wonders for organizing your time. Suddenly it becomes easy to say no, easy to fend off phone calls or unannounced visitors. Your mantra becomes, "I've got to get this done."

Then you start to play a little game. "I wonder if I can finish this by Wednesday instead of Friday. Then I could get a jump on project B." Suddenly you're chewing up work faster than ever, and people begin to marvel. (And perhaps pile more work on you.) You get known for producing, for being effective. Opportunities for promotions and other exciting endeavors start flying your way.

The truth is, you're not working that much harder or longer, if at all. You're not lugging your briefcase home each night. You are simply concentrating on important things that crowd out the unimportant.

You don't want more work? That's fine. As I said, this is a technique of achievers, those with more than a little ambition.

The Agile Manager's Checklist

✔ Discover where your time goes by keeping a time log.
✔ Plan your day using two essential tools: a to-do list and a calendar. (Fancy planners: optional.)
✔ Make lengthy appointments with yourself. This is when you'll get the most done.
✔ Set deadlines for yourself. Then move them up.

Chapter Four

Control the Paper In Your Life

There is one thing people could notice about the Agile Manager's desk if they bothered to take the time.

It didn't have any paper on it except for maybe one neat pile directly in front of him.

Not that it was clean as the flight deck of an aircraft carrier. There was a coffee cup and a small plant in one corner, and a few family pictures askew in the middle. A pen or pencil seemed to be within a few inches of wherever your hand may be. The telephone lay on three books, each set at different angles. At the rear of the right-hand side stood a wire rack that held six or seven manila folders marching upward. And the desk itself was old and battered, as if his grandfather had used it in the 1940s. (He had.)

You knew the Agile Manager was no everything-at-right-angles neat freak. But where was all the paper?

You can't get things done efficiently if you don't have a system for handling and storing paper and other documents that come across your desk. It's important to be able to put your hands on papers quickly, and to be able to switch gears quickly and start working on something else when you need to.

To do so, you need to keep related papers together. And you need to know how to find them.

Some experts say, "You should be able to put your hand on any piece of paper in your office in ten seconds or less." Some people probably can, but you wouldn't want to know them.

Close is good enough in paper-handling. As long as you can put your hand on anything in a minute or so, you're doing fine.

Be Able to Clear Your Desk

To do your best work, and to focus solely on the task at hand, be able clear your desk at a moment's notice. This provides a psychological benefit as well as a spatial one—you're cleared for takeoff.

Being able to clear your desk quickly requires knowing a few tricks. The first is to handle all paper in one location. Not one office, but one desk and an adjacent filing cabinet. You need a "command center" to force you to deal with inefficient piles (else how can you work at your desk?) and to limit the number of places paper can be.

Organize the Paper You Have

Trick number two is knowing how to organize the paper you now have. This is simple. You need a filing cabinet (or a filing crate if you want to save money), a box of manila folders, a box of hanging folders, and labels.

Go through all your loose paper. Put related items in a manila folder. Type or print neatly the folder's contents on a label. "Rivera Project," for example, or "Memos on Product X." If you need a series of folders for a particular project or subject, then group them together into a hanging file.

Unless you're now working on that folder or you work on it regularly, file it in the filing cabinet. If the file is going to grow, give it its own hanging file. If not, put it with other files that relate somehow. Call it something that you'll remember and that will remind you of what's inside. "New Product Warranties" is one example. "Information on NAFTA" is another.

Keep files in strict alphabetical sequence.

When naming files, don't follow anyone's suggestions but your own. Name them something descriptive and distinctive that will stick in your mind. If you ever have trouble finding a file, either fix it well in your mind or rename it.

Some people like to create an index of their file names so they can scan it before they get out of their chairs to find the file. If your labels remain neat and visible, I don't see the advantage. But maybe the idea appeals to you.

Handle all your paper in one location only. You need a command center to deal with it efficiently.

You also need a place to put files you're working on or those you consult frequently. Use the first position in the top drawer of your file cabinet. Better yet, buy a file rack that stands on the desktop. Quite handy, they come in wire or plastic format, and in various sizes. A desk rack keeps all the files you need for that day or that week within easy reach.

What about multitiered, horizontal trays? Hmm. They take up a lot of room, and they aren't that easy to access. (Ever try to find a piece of paper somewhere in the pile on the bottom tray?) You might use one as an in-box and maybe another as an out-box if you need it. But use them only for transitory items— never to store things longer than a day or two.

Handle Incoming Paper Efficiently

To handle new paper, first get a big garbage can (or maybe two—one for recycling). Second, do whatever it takes—a Post-it note stuck to your desk that says "Go ahead—toss it," or a visit to the shrink—to deflect most of the paper that comes into your life.

As you go through your mail, memos, and reports, ask yourself some questions:

1. *Do I really need to read or act on this?* If not, dump it immediately.

2. *Do I really need to keep this?* If not, dump it.

3. *Should someone else have this?* Send it on its way.

4. *If I need to keep it, must I keep it for a short time or permanently?* If it's for a short time, put it in a file on your desk called "Current" or something similar. If it's too bulky—like a magazine or a report—have one (and only one) reading pile. Go through both your current file and reading pile frequently and prune items from them as they lose value. If you need to keep an item for a longer time, create a file for it or file it with others of a similar nature.

5. *Do I need to act on this now?* Do so if you must—but very few things should fall into this category. If not, put it on your to-do list and file it where you'll remember it.

At times you'll agonize over whether you need to keep something or not. Ask yourself, "What could happen if I don't keep it?" Four times out of five you'll realize the paper is not all that important, or it's replaceable. If you're not sure, throw it into your current file. Time helps clarify the importance of things.

Should you touch paper only once? That's the guiding principle of many ruthless paper hounds.

|Best Tip

If you're wondering whether to keep a piece of paper, ask, "What's the worst that could happen if I don't keep it?"

I'm not with them on this. Sometimes an issue isn't ripe for action and you have to touch a paper many times before it comes alive. Sometimes you honestly don't know whether you should save something but have a sneaking suspicion that you should. Listen to your gut and keep the doubtful items in the "Current" file.

A final thought: *Deal with your paper in this way once every day.* If you're away for a few days, deal with it all at once. Don't let paper get the best of you.

Deal with the Dreaded Reading Pile

Every manager seems to have a foot-high pile of magazines, newspapers, newsletters, and briefings somewhere in the office. Some have a pile of similar height at home.

As the reading pile grows, so does the urge to banish it to the recycling bin in one fell swoop. Don't. There's gold in that pile. You just need to know how to find it.

Best Tip

Scan the contents of a magazine. Circle the items you really want to read. Read only those articles.

The problem with getting through the reading pile is that you pick up a magazine and get absorbed in it. You're only halfway through when reading time is over—and you have ninety-nine magazines to go.

The secret is to read selectively. Pick up a magazine and analyze the table of contents. Circle the articles you want to read, then go directly to those pages only. If you have to put the magazine down, be sure to consult the contents when you pick it up again. This one little trick will save you a lot of time.

If you're really overwhelmed, try the brute-force method: Take a pile of magazines and give yourself a certain amount of time to get through them. Find the articles you want to read and cut (or rip) them from the binding. Staple the pages and put the article into a manila folder. When time is up, recycle whatever is left over.

Before long, you'll have a custom selection of reading that's both pertinent and useful.

One last thing: Before you add an item to your reading pile, be absolutely certain it contains something you want to read.

Take a quick look at the contents or executive summary. If no article makes your pulse race a bit faster, dump it.

Stop the Urge to Force Paper on Others

Once you've tamed the paper tiger, take steps to ensure you don't inflict unnecessary paper on yourself or others:

- Don't print out an e-mail message unless it's absolutely necessary. (And use the same principles outlined above to file your e-mail on your hard drive.)
- Don't print out anything from your computer unless you must. The computer releases you from the burden of generating paper, especially when you're networked with other people or the outside world via a phone line. For example, if you can fax direct from your computer, why not do it? And don't print out drafts of anything. Use the same principles you learned above to file electronic documents. (Some people think this takes some special skill or magic. It doesn't. Your computer is an electronic filing cabinet that can be structured to mimic the five-foot cabinet at your elbow.)
- Don't "copy for the file" or make copies to cover your butt—unless you have good reasons for doing so.
- Don't add people to a distribution list for a regular report or memo unless they ask to be on it or they absolutely must be. And look for reasons to take people off a distribution list—or for your name to be taken off someone else's.

In short, question yourself closely every time you're about to generate paper.

Clean Out Your Files

Once a year, set aside a morning to go through your filing cabinet and desk drawers. Get rid of paper you don't need. A good rule of thumb: If you haven't looked at it for a year or more, dump it.

Take the opportunity to revise your filing system, too. Eliminate little-used categories, and add new ones or subcategories. A tip-off that a change is in order: Files that are either anorexic or obese.

This yearly ritual also results in finding buried treasure—paper you thought you lost, good ideas you'd written down and forgotten about, and reminders of past-year successes.

Slightly more often—say, every six months—go through your computer files and perform the same chore. This job takes more vigilance than cleaning your paper files. That's because paper never bulges out of a computer, and with a good "find" function you can usually find anything you need.

But you're getting organized, remember? And getting organized isn't a spot tool. It's a way of life.

Can You Survive Without Paper? Ask Insurer USAA

USAA specializes in insuring U.S. military officers, and it takes a dim view of paper. And why not? Storage costs for documents in paper form—especially for insurance companies, government agencies, and others—is huge.

A crew at USAA opens all policyholder mail—applications, address changes, claims correspondence, etc.—scans it into an electronic system, and then shreds it. They've been following this procedure since 1987.

Don't print out anything from your computer unless you must.

This philosophy is about more than just getting rid of paper. It streamlines and improves customer service. When a policyholder calls with a question or request, any of the company's 10,000 employees can call up customer-related correspondence in just five seconds. Saves time? You bet. At USAA, you'll never hear anyone say, "Let me pull that file and call you back."

This philosophy works at a personal level, too. I once spoke to a Silicon Valley executive who had banished paper from his

life. Completely. If he couldn't have it in some electronic format—disk, CD-ROM, or Web—he didn't want it. He was not, he
felt, missing a thing.

The Agile Manager's Checklist

✔ Once a day, act on the paper that comes into your life.
You can:

- ■ Trash it;
- ■ Send it to someone else;
- ■ File it;
- ■ Act on it.

✔ Don't add an item to your reading pile unless you're
absolutely sure it contains something of value. Place a
Post-it note to remind you where that value lies.
✔ Refrain from generating paper.
✔ Clean out your files once a year.
✔ Remember: It's possible to operate in paperless mode.

Chapter Five

Organize Your Work

The Agile Manager made the first of six phone calls to his mates on the new-product team.

"Chet," he said. "According to my schedule, today is the day you're supposed to have the preliminary cost figures drawn up on Project Simmer. I don't have them yet." Chet waited for him to continue, but the Agile Manager remained silent, gritting his teeth.

"Well, I thought it was tomorrow—late tomorrow."

"Nope." More silence.

"Well, I'll get them to you soon." Chet couldn't understand why he was unable to tell this guy to jump in the lake.

"Thanks," said the Agile Manager, who hung up and expelled a lungful of air.

"Maura," he said with the next call, "Your designs for stage one of Project Simmer were beautiful. Did I tell you that? I can't wait to see those for stage two."

"Oh, thanks. I got sidetracked but I'll get them to you tomorrow."

"Thanks."

"Harve," said the Agile Manager. "The marketing people are jerking me around about the compatibility issue with previous mod-

*els. Project Simmer I'm talking about. Weren't you going to talk
with them?"*

*"I talked to Gus, but I probably should've mentioned it to Martha.
I'll buzz her right now."*

"Thanks—and by the way, I shot an 82 at Oak Point yesterday . . ."

*And so it went. Steve was astonished regularly by the way the
Agile Manager managed projects. For one thing, he took a different tone and style with everyone he talked to. And no matter who
it was, he stayed on top of that person until he got what the group
needed. This was no easy feat, Steve knew, because the Agile
Manager outranked none of them officially. Yet he rarely missed a
deadline, and he frequently beat them by a wide margin.*

How can some people stay on top of their work so well that
they don't miss deadlines? Most have a system for organizing
and carrying out their assignments and long-term projects.

Complete an Assignment on Time

Let's take a simple example of how to get something done on
time. Say your boss walks in and tells you she wants a feasibility
study on entering the Mexican market by the end of next week.
Then she walks out without another word.

You've got two other projects going on, not to mention your
daily duties or the two people you supervise, so you begin to
panic.

Don't.

First sit down with a piece of paper or your word processor
and define the assignment in your own words. Do you know:

- What a feasibility study entails?
- What should be included?
- How wide a scope your boss wants?
- What kind of conclusion she's looking for?
- Why she wants one done? (The answer to that is a good
  way to establish a context for the work and how deep to
  go into it.)

Don't run back and forth to her office for answers—read up as much as you can and nose around for information from your work mates first. Part of carrying out a project usually involves helping define or flesh it out.

Next, briefly outline the information you're going to need and how you're going to get it.

At this point, write a short memo for your boss (or have a quick meeting) that covers what you believe are the key issues and how you're going to tackle the assignment. This gives her a chance to say, "Yes, sounds right," or "No, I was more interested in . . ."

You might also say something like, "Because you seem to be giving this a priority, I'm putting the benefits project on the back burner for a week or so." This reminds her you have other things going and makes sure everyone agrees the new assignment takes priority.

Now go over your outline again and make a real work plan from it. You'll need to gather information, analyze it, draw conclusions, and present your findings. Don't skimp at this stage; time spent planning is among the highest-leverage work you can do.

Next, sit down with your to-do list and calendar and create time for doing those tasks. Then do them.

If anything goes wrong, or if the process seems inefficient, conduct a post-assignment review: Where were the problems? How could I have avoided them? Could I have done better or worked faster? Should I have talked to other people? Where do my skills seem to lag?

Six steps, then, to complete an assignment successfully:

1. *Define the assignment in your own words.*
2. *Outline briefly how you'll do the work.*
3. *Check with the boss to make sure you're on track.*
4. *Plan your work in detail.*
5. *Do the work.*
6. *Review the work.*

As should be clear by now, organizing yourself and your work isn't brain surgery. It takes only the commitment to organize and plan, and the ability to follow a schedule.

Organize a Project

The basics for organizing a project expand on those for doing an assignment. But you have to do more planning to stay on schedule, and you also have one big added complication: other people.

Let's say your boss asks you to lead a project team to prepare a bid for getting a government contract. It could mean $4 million over five years for the company, so it's a big priority. The deadline, he says, is two months. Let's run through the steps.

Define the assignment. Put down on paper, in your own words, what needs to be done and what results the company wants. This step and those to follow will take a fair amount of your time, so plan well. The more you plan and organize, however, the more time and energy you save down the road.

Best Tip

Make sure your boss agrees with your definition of the project and its scope.

Outline how the work will be done. Think about the project broadly. What other functions are involved? How much research needs to be done? Where? What's the sequence of actions? It helps here to think of the final goal and work backwards.

Identify the people whom you'll need to help. If you have a choice about your teammates, think who would be best in each slot. Don't worry about whether they are actually available or willing.

Review with your boss your work thus far. Do a memo, but insist on a face-to-face meeting as well. A project is usually a big job; if you have to redefine the job well into the game, you'll waste time. Ask your boss to help you obtain the people you identified as the best suited for working on the project.

Meet with everyone on the team to come up with a plan.
As a group, refine your plan. (Meeting skills are essential; see chapter nine.) Run down your estimation of what needs to be done and ask for input. Make sure everyone agrees on the overall plan.

Best Tip

Get a project-management software program that can create Gantt charts.

Next, set milestones, which are deadlines for each stage of the project. Milestones are essential for keeping on track. Assuming the deadlines are reasonable, *hold them to be inviolable.* Projects lose steam quickly when you keep missing deadlines.

After the meeting, write a memo that clearly defines the schedule of events and who is responsible for what, and when. Consider getting a software program that can do Gantt charts. On the left-hand side of the scale are the steps you need to take. The scale along the bottom is time. The chart itself is made up of horizontal bars that show how long each step is supposed to take. (Some people prefer flow charts. It must be a matter of taste; I find them confusing.)

In your planner or calendar, mark down the milestones. Also, set a regular meeting schedule with the group to ensure things

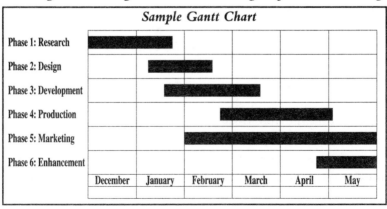

Sample Gantt Chart						
Phase 1: Research	███					
Phase 2: Design		███				
Phase 3: Development		███				
Phase 4: Production			███			
Phase 5: Marketing		███				
Phase 6: Enhancement					███	
	December	January	February	March	April	May

proceed smoothly. Set aside time for checking up on the progress of others.

Meet with the boss again to review the project. Especially if you've changed the plan from the last meeting. The group, for instance, may agree that the schedule you had envisioned is too tight to do a good job.

For important projects, schedule regular status meetings with your boss. Bosses can inform you of changes, for one thing, and they can help use their clout to get more resources or changes if necessary.

Best Tip
Whenever you're finished with a project, review the process and results. Each project offers an opportunity to improve your skills as well as your organizing methods.

Stay on top of people. People have a way of going off and doing their own thing after agreeing to the plan. In some cases you'll have the authority to get people to do your bidding, but more common these days is the team of peers. Learn to use all your political skills to influence people without annoying them.

If you feel you have no political skills, be sweet and charming. That goes a long way toward greasing the organizational wheels. Another good skill is simple persistence. When people discover you're not going to stop bothering them until they complete their tasks, they do the work just to get you off their backs. Finally, accommodate people. If you can help them out somewhere so they can get to the job you want done, do it.

Note: If you have trouble getting along with people, or getting things done through them, try a Dale Carnegie course in human relations. They really work.

Submit a final paper, bid, or presentation. The end of a project always culminates in some sort of finished work. Do your best here; I've seen a good end-of-project presentation win over people who were dead set against it based on the written report. (Chapter ten contains tips on creating an effective presentation.)

Review your work. Every project offers opportunities to improve your skills and the way you organize work. The best managers reflect on their jobs and how they accomplish work, always looking for ways to do better. It's a way to compile your own "book of wisdom" on management—and a way to give yourself an advantage when it comes time to get a better job.

Get Things in Motion

Besides having good people skills, if there's one secret to meeting your deadlines, it's this: Get activities in motion early. Begin with the items that take the most time.

Say, for instance, you have an assignment or project in which you'll need cost figures. You know one vendor takes three weeks to prepare a bid. So send that vendor the specs first. Or say a teammate in that project is always swamped with work. Take that into account; don't expect her to produce anything at a moment's notice. Get her moving first before you start working on the others.

Or say you know you want Smitty from accounting to be on a team given the job of overhauling compensation policies. He's really good. But everyone else knows he's really good, so he's in demand. If you know you'll need him in January, start working on him in late November and check in with him frequently: "Yeah, I just wanted to say that it looks like we're a go in the third or fourth week in January. I'll check back to verify that in a few weeks." Just make sure he doesn't forget.

To put things in motion effectively, it helps to have a plan of action drawn up. Gaze at it every so often and think, "How can I move on any of these items now?"

Find Time . . .

Another key to organizing excellence? Foresight. That takes uninterrupted blocks of time to plan and reflect. And you can't have uninterrupted blocks of time if you're always reacting to events or people around you.

The Agile Manager's Checklist

✔ Don't miss deadlines.

✔ To complete an assignment:

- Define the assignment.
- Outline briefly how you'll do the work.
- Check with the boss.
- Plan your work in detail.
- Do the work.
- Review the work.

✔ Don't forget: Your end-of-project presentation can make or break the project.

✔ Don't juggle tasks, but get as many in motion as you can as early as possible.

Chapter Six

Refresh Your Mind

Sometimes The Agile Manager went mid-morning. A few times a week he went at lunch. Once in a while he went late in the afternoon—and then came back into the office to confound those who suspected he wasn't putting in as many hours as they were. (He wasn't, of course.)

Steve, his assistant, believed he went to exercise, though all he ever said was, "I'm going out for a while." He came back showered and refreshed. Janet in marketing said she thought she saw him running one day but her colleague Hal said, no, that couldn't be; Hal understood that he'd ruined his knee playing rugby in college. (And Hal suspected he went out for another reason altogether—although he had to admit that even that was pretty good exercise.)

Whatever he did, thought Steve, it worked. He always came back smiling or whistling, and with a healthy glow. He'd then attack his work with gusto.

Down the hall sat Will, who resented it every time he saw the Agile Manager walk past his door and out of the building. "I work harder and longer than that guy," he often thought. "How come someone doesn't put the squeeze on him?"

You want to be better organized at work? Here are three secrets:

Secret #1: Don't Work So Much

Parkinson was absolutely right: Work expands to fill the time you give it, so it may seem like you're always doing something important and maybe getting more done when you spend long hours on the job. You're probably not. Full-blown workaholics do two things very well: Arrange masses of paper on their desks creatively, and hold fast to the attitude, "I can always get to it later. After all, I'll still be here."

It's rare to meet a workaholic who works smart. "Plan? Why do that? I'm here all the time anyway. Whatever it is, it'll get done." Or, "Think ahead? Why? I'm plugged in to this place. I know what I have to do."

Non-planners, in fact, make great workaholics: they don't prioritize or otherwise rank their duties. So they either try to do them all at the same time, or they put great energy and concentration into insipid activities like scheduling the use of the company tennis courts.

You workaholics are no doubt thinking, "You don't know what it's like around here. I have to work sixty-five hours a week just to stay ahead. Besides, everyone else does it, too." Ah, the big culprit: Peer pressure, usually inspired by a senior workaholic.

If you want to be like everyone else at your workaholic company, always looking tired and unhappy—and sometimes dying young—go ahead. But the truth is, for all but a chosen few, who arrived in the world wired with high-voltage systems, your ability to work deteriorates after a certain number of hours. (Ten is about maximum.) After that, you're doing neither yourself or your company any good.

If you work at a place that really requires sixty hours a week or more on the job . . . think hard about what you're getting out of it. Because when you factor in your commute, you don't have much of a life outside of work. (You may have a case against me if you're an investment banker who works ninety hours a week in exchange for the chance to retire at age twenty-eight.)

Secret #2: Get a Hobby

Do something—anything—that will divert your mind from work completely. The benefits are twofold: First, while you busy yourself with something else you enjoy, your magical unconscious mind, free of your conscious attention, will busy itself solving your problems, providing insights, relaxing you, and offering a fresh perspective once you return to your main job in life. You work better and faster.

Former Gen. Colin Powell, for instance, worked on old Volvos as a hobby. He liked the "certainty" represented by the nuts and bolts. It counterbalanced the uncertainty he felt in his work at the Pentagon.

The other benefit is that you gain knowledge in an area that could fertilize your thinking at work. For example, solving a problem in your hydroponic tomato shed at home might suddenly shed light on a problem at work. Or striving to understand how an electronic circuit conducts energy may help you solve a staffing problem in your department.

The best managers have a wide-ranging knowledge and a wide curiosity about life. If they want to learn about leadership, they are as apt to pick up a book on Lincoln or Churchill as they are a business book devoted to the subject. And they know that learning to reckon latitude by the stars or identifying birds or restoring old Packards has benefits far beyond the enjoyment yielded by the moment.

Secret #3: Exercise, Nap—and Play

Get off your butt, put out the cigarette, and go do a few laps around the park. Or get out on the golf course (no carts). It'll make you feel great, and it's the best stress-buster you'll ever find. (Have a runner tell you about the kick endorphins provide.) The key is to make it a regular practice.

Even if you can't leave the office midday to exercise, you can still refresh yourself. One way is to meditate or take a nap. Either could be dangerous if you work in a large office with open cubicles. But can't you sneak off somewhere? Even a five-minute cat nap rejuvenates you considerably.

Many senior executives well understand the benefit of a short nap in the afternoon. They happily settle onto their office couches around 1:30 P.M.—because they can. It'd be nice to see more corporate-sanctioned sleeping on the job. Productivity would rise.

Another way to freshen your mind and body is to have an office well-stocked with toys. A gun with squishy darts is fun, as are small puppets, windup toys, and those games in which you try to get beads through a maze or into a hole.

If you work for a humorless organization, keep the toys out of sight.

Plan Your Day According to Cycles

Are you a morning person or an evening person? You probably answered that immediately.

Keep your "type" in mind when planning. Arrange things to suit your schedule. You have a big negotiation coming up? Do it when you're at your best. Or travel during your down times.

It's unfortunate that "face-time" in corporate America primarily means staying late at the office. Those who come in extra-early rarely get the credit they deserve. Working without interruption after a good night's sleep, early birds are likely more productive than others.

The Agile Manager's Checklist

✔ Don't work so much.
✔ Get a hobby.
✔ Exercise regularly.
✔ Use toys and relaxation methods at work to refresh yourself.
✔ Plan your day to take advantage of energy cycles.

SECTION III

Eliminate Time-Wasters

"For one either meets, or one works."

— Peter F. Drucker
in *The Effective Executive*

Chapter Seven

Defang the Deadliest Time-Wasters

Steve came in mid-morning as usual on Mondays with an armful of reports, memos, and other documents.

"Where do you want these?" he asked the Agile Manager.

"Square in the middle of the desk. I'll deal with them right now."

When Steve came back with a few messages an hour later, the three-inch pile of reports had become only a quarter-inch high. The Agile Manager was concentrating so deeply on one report, a spreadsheet of some kind, that he didn't see Steve return.

Steve flipped the messages on the desk and left. On his way out, he noticed at least half the reports he'd brought in that morning lying in the recycling bin; one big report still had a foil seal around it. The Agile Manager hadn't even looked at it.

"So much work, such little effect," thought Steve.

Time-wasters are the biggest enemy of your organization and your effort to manage time. Let's go through the worst offenders one by one to see how you can keep them from ruining your day. Before we begin, it should be said that some pruning activity may interfere with your corporate culture and levels of authority. If your boss, or your boss's boss, wants you to do unnecessary work, then you have to do it. But you might think about migrating to a more productive workplace.

Time-waster #1: Meetings. These are among the worst threats to managing your time. Once people get together, it takes great effort to separate them. And there go two hours of perfectly good time.

Many meetings are necessary. Some are quite useful. At least half are neither. We have far too many of them, and most are so poorly run that whatever value they may have had soon disappears.

Chapter nine shows you how to decide whether to hold a meeting, and how to conduct an effective one when you do. Read it well so you don't waste the time of others and join with the mediocre in ruining the company's productivity.

Best Tip
Ask yourself, "Do I really have to attend this meeting?" If so, can you limit the time you spend at it?

Don't automatically give in to those who try to cram their meetings into your schedule. Ask:

1. Do I have to attend?
2. If I must attend, can I limit the time I spend there?
3. What can I personally do to ensure an effective meeting? For instance, ask for an agenda so you can prepare. (The meeting initiator's probable response: "An agenda? Am I supposed to have an agenda? I didn't know.") If there's not a stated goal for the meeting, shame the person who called it into formulating one.

In the worst case, you have to attend a meeting you know will turn out to be a total time-waster. If possible, remain respectfully aloof so people know you're not there to talk about day-care or why the senior vice president got fired. If you're lucky, people will decide you're a threat to their desire to waste a few hours and stop inviting you to their meetings.

Using your best political skills, question the value of these kinds of meetings:

Regular meetings. "We always have a meeting at 10:00 A.M. on Tuesday." Why? Do you still need one? Sometimes merely asking the question is enough to change tradition.

Status meetings. Can e-mail inform people better, or a regular memo routed to key people? The worst is having a meeting when nothing has changed.

"Pep" meetings. Some managers hold these meetings for no other reason than to congratulate one another for work well done. It's supposed to be a good way to motivate people. I doubt it works.

In the meetings you lead, and the meetings you attend, demand value. Even if you become known as a curmudgeon. If nothing else, people might stop asking you to attend senseless meetings.

Time-waster #2: Unnecessary reports and memos you must read. Especially in larger organizations, there is much "legacy" work. Your department has always received such-and-such report, where it is to be filed in a big black binder and never looked at. Or a certain document has always been routed to the person in your job for review.

There was probably a good reason once for you or your department to receive any regular communication. But these reasons get lost over time. That's why you question everything routed your way. If something is clearly

Best Tip
If you're not getting any feedback on the reports you're doing, stop preparing them and see who squawks.

unnecessary in your job, and you can get away with it, ask to be removed from the distribution list. You can camouflage your actions by saying something like, "Maybe Jill over in marketing would profit by it more." (But do Jill a favor and be sure she actually could profit by it.)

Even worthwhile documents are time-consuming. Can you get an assistant or someone else to read a report and summarize the highlights for you?

Caution: It's human nature to want to be involved, to want to know what's going on around the organization. It's also human nature to feel you may fall "out of the loop" if you stop looking at certain reports or regular memos. Guarding your time is more important than assuaging your ego.

If you stop looking at things that don't concern you, and invest the extra time in doing your job more effectively, being "out of the loop" will never be a problem for you.

Time-waster #3: Unnecessary reports and memos you must write. Sometimes you inherit the job of producing a document because a) the document has always been produced, and b) your department has always done it. Whatever the reason, it takes you three hours a week, and additional administrative time for copying, routing, etc., to get the report out. What a productivity killer!

Nose around to see who still reads the report. You may find that people find it useful. Then keep on producing it, with joy in your heart. If no one reads it, and you're feeling bold, you might ask your boss directly whether the report still needs to be done. Before you do, make fairly certain the answer will be "no." And be prepared to explain why you think it should be scrapped.

A more subversive method is to stop doing the report and see what happens. If anyone calls looking for it, you can say you're running late and you'll get it out right away.

Reports from the field, however, indicate this tactic can be dangerous. A highly placed executive might batch reports and read them regularly but at, say, three-month intervals. So you may forget all about the report and then get smacked hard for not having done it.

Time-waster #4: Unnecessarily good reports and presentations. Some corporate cultures place as much emphasis on how you present your findings and recommendations as they do on the findings themselves. As a result, otherwise productive workers spend late nights and weekends touching up slides, practicing presentations endlessly, or tinkering to find just the right font for their reports. All of this comes at a huge cost to the organization, of course.

Ask yourself: Do your superiors really value such effort? Or is it a competition among peers?

Quality, remember, doesn't mean "all the bells and whistles." It means fitness for use. Quality is what gets the job done and nothing more.

In any report, verbal or written, get to the point as quickly and simply as possible. That's what people want to hear. Does a multimedia presentation help you get to the point any faster? Often it does just the opposite.

Time-waster #5: Unnecessary travel. Business people like to complain about the rigors of traveling. But they must like it at some level to endure the discomforts as frequently as they do. Or maybe it makes them feel they are doing something.

Is a forty-five minute meeting in a distant city really worth the price of a full-day's disruption to your life and schedule? Some-

| **Best Tip**

Always ask, "Could e-mail or a videoconference substitute for travel?"

times it is. But ask yourself, at least, whether a telephone call, a videoconference, or an e-mail conversation wouldn't suffice.

Time-waster #6: Unnecessary lunches/functions. You may think you need to go out to lunch with someone, or attend a dinner or other function, but do you? Imagine what would happen if you declined a lunch invitation or missed an industry function. Would the world cave in? If so, go. But you might miss a few just to see what happens. (A secret: People often invite you to things to be polite. They won't be at all disappointed when you decline.)

Time-waster #7: Commuting. What could be a bigger waste of time than sitting in traffic or standing flattened inside a train car twice a day? Just imagine if you could stay home one day a week, or maybe a couple of mornings. Employers are becoming more receptive to the idea that you can be more productive away from the office than in it.

If you can't avoid a commute (and it may be worth changing jobs for a saner schedule), at least make it productive. Listen to books on tape or car pool with an intelligent friend.

Time-waster #8: Waiting to get finished work. If others are lagging in their commitments to you, bug them until you get what you need. Be nice, be courteous, but be persistent until they fulfill their obligations. You may become known as a pest, but you'll usually get what you want.

Time-waster #9: Waiting for others. Say a group of people constantly show up late for meetings. Or a friend is never on time for lunch. Do as Dale Carnegie suggests and put a "stop-loss" order on your time. If you have a meeting at 10:00 A.M., vow to leave by 10:10 if no one shows up by then. Give your lunch date ten or fifteen minutes, but limit your losses. Your co-workers and friends will soon learn to respect the clock. If you've been wimpy, this little trick can gain you a couple of extra hours a week.

| Best Tip

Every so often, decline an invitation to attend a luncheon or other business function. The world won't fall in.

Time-waster #10: People who waste your time. They waste your time on the telephone, they waltz into your office unannounced, they want appointments with you for no good reason, they stay too long after business has been conducted, and they pepper you with e-mail on petty subjects. You must stop them.

To ward people off politely sometimes takes subterfuge. Helen Gurley Brown, former editor of *Cosmopolitan* magazine, never granted an appointment until she knew exactly what the person wanted.

When she saw someone, she determined in advance how much time the appointment should take. Then she arranged to have her assistant pop her head in the door at the predetermined time and say, "Ms. Brown, you're needed in the art department."

Best Tip

When you want to end a personal meeting, stand up, grin, stick out your hand, and say, "Great talking with you!"

At the very least, learn to stand up, smile broadly, stick out your hand, and say, "Great talking with you! Now I've got some other things to attend to." On the telephone, use the old standby, "I won't keep you any longer. I'm sure you have things to do," and hang up.

To deal with pernicious e-mailers, don't respond. Even when they ask, "Did you get my last message?"

Time-waster #11: Telephone tag. This is becoming rarer thanks to voice mail. But if you find yourself feeling like a Ping-Pong ball, tell the person to call at a time you know you will be available.

Time-waster #12: Socializing. The people who get ahead on the job stick to it. They socialize just enough to seem civil, and sometimes with great charm, but they do just enough and no more. (They save themselves for times they can pour it on thick—lunch and other functions.)

If you've been in the work world for a while, you know that watercooler schmoozers don't have great career prospects. For political reasons, you'll want a nodding acquaintance with those content to wile away their time in idle patter, but, generally, stay away.

Time-waster #13: Shifting priorities. You've put in two weeks of hard work on the Berman account when the boss yanks you off it and puts you on the Schwartz account instead. Or you devote nine months to a new-product effort when senior managers suddenly pull the plug.

Such events hurt. And they don't do your career much good. After all, how can you share in the glory of a new product that never makes it into daylight?

Though there's often not much you can do, keeping your ear to the ground can help you anticipate problems. You can sense if a project is in trouble, for example, when a routine request for funds gets stalled. Or if your boss becomes evasive on certain aspects of the project. If you know the work you're doing is doomed, maybe you can find a way to abandon ship before the end.

| **Best Tip**
|
| If your boss suddenly becomes evasive about a long-term project you're working on, beware. It may be on the chopping block.

Time-waster #14: Poor communication. Experts say billions of dollars are lost each day due to poor communications. How often does a memo leave you bewildered? ("What exactly is the point?") How often does a superior confuse you? ("What exactly am I supposed to do?") All communication is two-way, of course. And poor listening is at least as big a productivity-killer as poor writing or directions.

There's another factor. Humans are unpredictable. As management consultant Richard Moran puts it, "Never underestimate the ability of people to develop strange interpretations of anything you write, say, or do."

Always strive to ensure that you are understood by others, and that you understand what others are communicating to you. If in doubt, check. I once had a supervisor absolutely incapable of offering a clear direction. So I learned to boil down and synthesize what I heard and regurgitate it immediately: "So you want me to deal with problem x right now, then get back to project y?"

Don't waste one minute wondering what people mean. Ask again if necessary. Your effectiveness depends on it.

Time-waster #15: Indecision. This, remember, is one of the roots of clutter. And clutter is a root cause of wasted time. If you've created goals for yourself, and if you know what's expected of you at work, then you can eliminate most indecision.

The rest probably has to do with your fear, uncertainty, and doubt (FUD) regarding an issue. That uncertainty can incapacitate you. (FUD, incidentally, can also incapacitate an entire organization.)

To make a decision,

- Define the problem clearly and succinctly, making sure you are treating the real problem and not its symptoms.
- Get as much pertinent information as you can. (Put a limit on either the time you spend or the information you amass, because you can go on collecting information forever.)
- Analyze the information.
- Take a stand.

Remember, making the wrong decision is usually better than doing nothing. And it's rarely the end of the world. (Sometimes doing nothing *is* the right decision. But make it a conscious choice.)

Time-waster #16: Perfectionism. It often takes 50 percent or more of the total effort to squeeze out that last 10 percent or so of quality or whatever it is perfectionists want out of a situation. Many workaholics are part-time perfectionists, making it even harder for them to get home at a decent hour.

Perfection is rarely required. And it sucks up time voraciously. Learn when to say "good enough," even it if it takes professional counseling to do so.

Best Tip

Avoid perfectionism. It'll take you 50 percent of the total effort to squeeze out that last 10 percent of quality.

Time-waster #17: Fatigue. You don't work efficiently when you're tired. So you end up working longer—and get even more tired. Go back and reread the last chapter if this is a problem for you.

Time-waster #18: Attempting to do too much. Many disorganized people have great ambitions. They have numerous projects going at once, and before they finish even one they're off concocting others. The results of their stalled efforts lie around them as reminders of unfinished business. This would depress most of us, but dreamers are too busy with new plans to care.

If you want to be effective and use your time smartly, pick a few projects and complete them. Then pick more and complete those. This book has given you the tools to do both.

Time-waster #19: Procrastination. This isn't the place to go into why you procrastinate, except to say you've probably allowed a project or activity to loom too large in your mind. The mere thought of tackling it overwhelms you.

One way to deal with procrastination is to set aside time in your planner to finish the activity. If you find you can't take even that modest step, try this: Work on the project for ten minutes only. (Use a watch or timer to gauge the time.) Once you get into it, you may find yourself happy to continue for an hour or more. You may even decide to finish it altogether. But if you can stomach only ten minutes, at least you're that much closer to completion.

The reason this technique works is simple: Procrastination is often the inability to get started. Once you do, you'll find it easy to keep moving until your task is completed.

The Agile Manager's Checklist

✔ Avoid meetings you know serve no purpose.
✔ Get unnecessary reports out of your life.
✔ Do just "good enough" with the reports and presentations you must create.
✔ Don't wait more than ten minutes for people to show up for a meeting or a lunch date.
✔ Make decisions quickly. Even if you decide wrong, it's better than being indecisive.
✔ When procrastinating, decide to spend just ten minutes at the task you're avoiding.

SECTION IV

Leverage Yourself

"There are two levers for moving men—interest and fear."

— NAPOLEON BONAPARTE

Chapter Eight

Delegate!

The Agile Manager walked out of his office and sat down next to Steve.

"I have some things I want you to do," he said. "This one is easy. I'm supposed to do a report of expenses related to the Van Paten alliance project every two weeks. I've done the first one — here it is so you understand the format.

I'll keep the expenses — mostly invoices and receipts — in a file called "Alliance" that sits on my desk. Just grab that file every two weeks, do the report, and send it to these people." The Agile Manager handed Steve a list. "Any questions?"

"No."

"The second thing is more complicated. Skillful as I am, I can't be everywhere at once. Yet every Tuesday for the next two months, I'm supposed to be attending three meetings — two here in the building at 10:00 A.M., and one across town at VentureCorp at 10:30. I can't get out of any of them. So I want you to be me for a while every Tuesday. Here's how we'll do it and what I want from you . . ."

As the Agile Manager talked, Steve marveled again at how his mind worked and how he got away with things that most managers would never try. But that was the key, Steve realized. You have to try.

Many managers miss huge opportunities to create time they can devote to truly important activities. These are the many opportunities you have to delegate your tasks, from the mundane to the important, to subordinates.

Contrary to what some people will tell you, however, your ultimate goal as a manager isn't to supervise only and do zero work. It's hard to achieve that golden state, for one thing. But even if you could, you wouldn't gain much respect. Your troops want to see you slogging along in the trenches with them.

Yet you have many chances to get out from under noncritical, if not inconsequential, work. The best managers make the most of such opportunities.

Managers often don't delegate because they:

- Rationalize that it would take longer to explain a job than to do it themselves;
- Don't think the staff has the right skills;
- Don't believe the staff will take on responsibility and accountability;
- Are afraid of what would happen if the subordinate failed;
- Like to do certain tasks, even if others could do them;
- Are simply afraid of teaching subordinates how to do their jobs. It's threatening.

Best Tip

When looking for things to delegate, start with recurring tasks you consider administrative chores.

All these reasons stink. Remember the big picture: You should lust for anything that will give you extra, quality time to really contribute to the organization and its goals. That's what you're there for. That's what you'll be rewarded for.

Besides, delegating is a great way to keep the troops happy and feeling empowered. People love to do significant things, especially if they help them grow and increase their self-confidence.

In short, you're doing everyone a service when you delegate.

What to Delegate

Look over your to-do list for the day, together with the things you know you have to do for the month. Begin by looking for recurring things you consider chores. Maybe you have to prepare a report each month, attend regular meetings, or file documents with the government. Maybe there's burdensome reading—for instance, you have to follow regulatory rulings. Delegate as many of these things as you can.

But consider delegating just about anything—compiling special reports or studies, meetings with other firms or departments you're working with, and so on.

You shouldn't, of course, delegate confidential things, like dealing with employee problems. Nor should you delegate planning or strategizing (else why does the company need you?) or those things in which you deliver unique value. Generally, keep the highest priority items for yourself, and delegate the rest.

Pick the Right Person

Now think about your people. Don't look for the nearest warm body to toss work to. The general rule of thumb is to delegate to the most junior person who is able to do the job. That's the person making the least amount of money and doing things of lesser importance. This frees up everybody above that person to concentrate on higher-order items.

You have to make sure the person has the clout to get the job done, however, so sometimes you'll need to use a person of a certain rank or level of personal authority.

Sometimes you can hand things off laterally to another department or peer, but be prepared to offer something in exchange. Usually, however, you'll be delegating to those directly subordinate to you.

Define the Job and the Result You Want

Define clearly what you want done and the results you expect. Help the employee by putting the job in context. ("By doing this research, you'll help me prepare a report I have to give to the Product Development Committee on the effectiveness of using outside designers.")

Be sure to explain your standards, especially the degree of detail you want, and how polished the work should be. And provide a firm deadline.

Outline, too, the level of autonomy you're giving the person. This depends on the job and person. Lower-level people in new tasks may require a fair amount of guidance at regular intervals. But beware this doesn't descend into hand-holding or you'll lose the value of delegating. With such people you'll say, "Check in with me every Tuesday to tell me what's doing on." With some higher-level, highly competent people, you can simply say, "Go do a good job and come back when you're done."

> ## Best Tip
>
> When delegating, don't tell people how to do the job. Tell them what results you want.

If at all possible, don't tell the person *how* to do the job. Part of the fun, and the growth opportunity, lies in figuring that out. Besides, maybe they'll do it a better way than you would.

Having done all that, make absolutely sure people understand the job and your expectations. If necessary, have them repeat it back to you or write it out in their own words.

Check In

If the task will take time, check in periodically to see how things are going. This doesn't mean interfere or offer help where it isn't needed. Rather, it's a way to ensure things are on schedule and that the person isn't lacking necessary resources to finish on time.

For most projects, check in informally. If a project is complicated or lengthy, you may want regular feedback. This can be in the form of a weekly memo, a brief meeting, or phone call.

If you've delegated a recurring task and the person is doing a good job, forget about it.

Evaluate

Like all other areas of management, delegating is something you get better at with time. With experience, you'll know better which things to delegate, understand the capabilities of your people, and gain a sense of when your help is needed. But to get these benefits, you should evaluate—mentally, at least—how well each delegating event came off. Ask:

1. Did I get the desired result?
2. Did the person I delegated the job to grow and expand his or her capacity to accept responsibility?
3. Did I keep out of the person's way?
4. Did I increase the confidence I have in my staff?
5. Did I successfully leverage myself?

A "no" to any of these questions calls for analysis.

Problems in Delegating

Some problems seem to recur in delegating.

The job gets delegated back. There are people out there with a real skill for resisting work, even when the boss asks for it. If you're not careful, they'll delegate work back to you faster than you know what hit you.

For instance, I once asked a person to gather some cost figures from a variety of sources. This wasn't difficult work, just time-consuming. Before I knew it, I was the one on the phone getting these figures. The person—a subordinate—had successfully delegated the job back to me.

Usually the subordinate will feign ignorance, purposely fumble the work, or protest that he or she doesn't have enough time. Here's one of the few cases where you must remember who the boss is. You're passing along work so you can better contribute to the firm. If you've chosen the person best able to get the job done, make sure he or she does it to completion.

The person is genuinely unable to do the work. Sometimes you choose the wrong person. Or maybe it's the right person with the wrong skills. If it's a recurring task, take the time to train that person. Doing so will save you loads of time later. Even if it's not a recurring task, consider doing the necessary training. It may still save you time, or it might give the person confidence and useful skills you can employ later.

"He's not doing it right." This is a problem in the mind of the delegator. You're not really letting go. Letting go is hard when you like the task and do it well. You naturally want to see someone perform to your standards. And you probably think people should do something just the way you do it.

As an old carpenter once told me, "There's more than one way to saw a board." Give people room to get the job done. You may be surprised at how it turns out.

You didn't get the right result. If you defined the task and your expectations properly, if you chose the right person, and if you checked in periodically, there's no reason the project should have failed. Look in the mirror before you blame someone else. And do better next time.

The Agile Manager's Checklist

✔ Examine your reasons for resisting delegating. Know that most of them are bogus.

✔ Delegate to keep people motivated.

✔ Delegate recurring chores like preparing reports, attending meetings, etc.

✔ Delegate to the lowest (i.e., least expensive) level you can.

✔ Define carefully the job you're delegating. Define even more carefully the result you want.

✔ Resist your temptation to interfere with, or take back, a job.

Chapter Nine

*P*lan and Lead
Effective Meetings

The Agile Manager sat at his desk, the late afternoon sun illuminating him.

He pondered whom to invite to a meeting next week on finding the causes of January's dismal sales figures. His boss, who would normally preside over a meeting of this importance, was attending a month-long program at Wharton. He had entrusted the whole thing to the Agile Manager.

The Agile Manager, as ever, refused to simply stand in for the boss. He used unusual events like this one to stretch himself, test his ideas about management, and learn.

Hmm, he thought. Ed would expect to be invited. But he talks too much, so no. He'll feel slighted, but this issue is too important for me to care. But he'll pay me back, for sure. Jill has a knack for getting to the heart of the matter. Yes. José's analytical mind would be indispensable here. Yes. Jack? Blustery. Hates it when anyone disagrees with him. But he knows the sales territories better than anyone. Yes. . . .

Okay, that makes six. Seven with me. All I want. Any more would ruin a meeting of this kind. But the boss always invited his four superiors. They rarely show but might send representatives. How can I finesse this?

The Agile Manager propped his feet on the desk and stared at a crack in the ceiling.

Got it, he thought. I'll invite them—sort of—while suggesting they'd probably find the complete summary I'll have for them the next day more useful. And a killer summary it will be. Now, how to word that "invitation" . . .

Poorly run meetings are among the greatest productivity killers known to mankind. Some managers, reportedly, spend 75 percent of their time in meetings. Don't they have jobs to do? Obviously, spending an inordinate amount of time in meetings controlled by others busts even the most carefully laid plans to manage time wisely.

Even "good" meetings threaten productivity. As Peter Drucker points out, "Meetings are by definition a concession to deficient organization." We hold them to coordinate work and exchange information—not perform work itself.

This chapter is about how you can take a personal role in combating the ills most meetings inflict on organizations by practicing good meeting skills. Such skills are a good way to leverage yourself by getting more done with the aid of others.

Should I Call a Meeting?

Your first question, always: "Do we need to meet?" The alternatives:

- Make a decision or do work on your own that eliminates the need to meet.
- Route a memo.
- Chat briefly and informally with a number of people on an issue and broadcast the results via report, e-mail, or memo.

You also have to fight your own urge to get together with people when it's not necessary. Regular weekly meetings often degenerate into unstructured bull sessions in which nothing is accomplished. The only antidote is to cancel the meeting.

If you must meet, follow the guidelines below.

Know What You Want to Accomplish

Be very clear about what you're trying to do by calling a meeting. Make a decision? Come up with a recommendation? Explore an issue? You're on the right track when the purpose of the meeting is to come up with some concrete, beneficial result that contributes to the overall goals of the organization.

Invite the Right People

Try to keep your meeting to no more than six to eight people. Any more and most of the participants don't get a good opportunity to air their views. People spout rather than discuss. And larger crowds encourage some to perform rather than think.

Choose participants carefully. Among the criteria:

- Invite those with essential information/expertise/background.
- Invite those directly affected.
- Invite those with exceptionally good analytical skills in areas germane to the topic.
- Invite those with political clout, if necessary.

Others will come to mind. Some may be outside the firm, like representatives from vendor companies or consultants. Avoid, if possible, those who like to show off, the argumentative, and those fundamentally unable to stay on track.

Circulate the Agenda

After inviting people to the meeting, write an agenda for it. At the top of the agenda, state what the meeting should accomplish. ("Purpose: To decide whether to go forward with producing the Microbot.") Remind people to bring special material if necessary, and let them know if they will be expected to speak at length for any reason.

Some people circulate an agenda a week beforehand. That's too long—people will lose it or forget about it. A day or two in advance is early enough.

Lead the Meeting

If a meeting is to succeed, it needs a leader. That's you. It's your job to make sure you get results. To do that:

- *Set a time limit and announce it at the beginning.* "I think we can get through this agenda in forty-five minutes. I promise to have you out of here at 2:45." This puts everyone on notice that the clock is ticking.

- *Take minutes or, preferably, designate someone else secretary.* Let people know they'll get a summary of the meeting within a day. That way they can concentrate on discussing, not note-taking.

- *Stick to the agenda.* Consider it inviolable. Give a certain amount of time to each item and check your watch regularly. If you don't, either the meeting will run over or you won't accomplish your purpose. (How often have you been to a meeting in which the whole time was taken up by just two of many agenda items?)

- *Lead by redirecting conversation when necessary.* "That's pretty interesting, Lenny. I'd love to discuss it with you sometime. Getting back to the problem at hand . . ." Sometimes you have to be rude if people are going on and on. "Thanks Carmine. Can we hear from someone else on this?"

Set a time limit for a meeting and stick to it.

Directing discussion in a meeting takes skill, diplomacy, and tact. But it's an ability that will serve you well.

- *Encourage productive discussion.* Here you need to be like the wise teacher needling her students to come to a truth on their own. "I hadn't thought of that, Denise. If we apply it to the warehouse bottleneck, are we any closer to a solution?" Also, if a key participant is holding back, bring her into the discussion. "Given your background in metallurgy, Jen, does that make sense?" But the idea isn't to bring others around to your point of view. Meetings should challenge the thinking of all participants.

Note: Peter Drucker believes it's impossible to both direct and participate in a meeting. He's probably right, but the practical reality is that you often have to do both.

Summarize, Come to a Conclusion, and Call for Action

If you're successful, the meeting will have come to a useful conclusion. End the meeting by summarizing the discussion and stating the conclusion: "John's evidence, I think, shows persuasively that there is a market for the Microbot. Agnes proved we could manufacture it without buying new equipment, and Mark seemed thrilled with the marketing angles the product provides. So we're agreed: We move forward to the prototype stage."

End the meeting by summarizing the discussion and stating a conclusion.

You can be sure anyone who doesn't see things your way will jump in: "I didn't say we wouldn't have to buy *any* new equipment—just nothing major. But I'm still in favor of it."

Now's the time also to remind people of their commitments. "For the next meeting, Thursday at 2:00, Agnes will provide a design spec for the Microbot, Mark will sketch out a preliminary space ad, and John will give his opinion on pricing options. Any questions?"

Send Along the Results

Within a day, send a copy of the meeting's minutes and conclusions to each participant. Be sure to include their commitments going forward and when the next meeting will take place.

If you want results, you must follow up on these commitments. Just because they are priorities to you doesn't mean they are priorities to anyone else—especially if the meeting included people from other companies.

As usual, take time to review how things went. Leading meetings is a tough job, but one you can get better at—to your great benefit.

The Agile Manager's Checklist

✔ Before you call a meeting, explore whether there is another way you can accomplish your purpose.

✔ Keep meetings to six participants or less. The fewer the better.

✔ Circulate an agenda before the meeting, and the minutes afterward.

✔ Never end a meeting without summarizing its findings and calling for more action if necessary.

Chapter Ten

Communicate with Skill

The Agile Manager looked down at the outline for the tenth time and once again went through the introduction and conclusion to the presentation. Tomorrow was the day—he would present the findings of his yearlong project on determining the prospects of Project Simmer to a group of about forty people, including the division general manager.

On the other side of the door, Steve heard the Agile Manager mumbling and knew he was practicing for the big presentation tomorrow. Steve was surprised when he decided on his own to present the findings to a large group. Steve himself was terrified of speaking to more than a couple people at once, and he knew that 75 percent of all the other managers were as well. Some would hide their fear by saying things like, "I prefer to present findings in written form. I think it conveys the depth of the issue better." Or, "I like to talk to people one-on-one so I get personal reactions."

Once Steve said to the Agile Manager, "Why do you willingly give presentations like these, especially when headquarters people are present? Aren't you scared?"

"Of course I'm scared. That's one reason I do it." Steve looked at him blankly, wondering if that were an explanation. "The other *reason is more practical. You work on a big project and a lot of people want to know about it. They call you, stop you in the hall, invite you to their meetings, ask you to write it up for part of a plan they are doing, and so forth. In other words, people take up tons of your time and you repeat things over and over. This way, I broadcast the material to all the people who need or want to know about it. Then I answer their questions about it. Then it's over, and I can get on with the project itself or with other things. If they missed the presentation and want information, I give them the handouts. If that's not enough, too bad."*

"Oh." Steve, as usual, hadn't considered an angle that seemed crystal clear to the Agile Manager.

Part of getting organized—part of getting ahead—is the ability to communicate effectively and broadly.

Communicating effectively is a time-management issue. If you can learn to be stunningly clear in all your communications (and few people are), you'll make a point well and once. Poor communicators create confusion: "What did she mean by that? Am I doing this right? I better go ask her."

Communicating broadly is also a time-management issue, because if you can reach a lot of people at once, they won't pester you for information one by one.

Presentations and Speeches

Smart managers don't hesitate to speak to groups when asked. They know that in the end it saves time.

Organizing and delivering a speech also sharpens communication skills—especially your ability to be clear and precise in making suggestions and recommendations, and in giving directions. It improves the valuable ability to think on your feet. And it gives you an opportunity to shine in front of the right people.

As a rule of thumb, plan to spend ten times the length of your presentation in preparing for it. Drafting notes or an outline is only part of the process; the rest is rehearsing it. Experienced presenters know that words convey only a small part of the message. You convey the rest through your gestures, props, and vocal inflections.

When you make a speech or give a presentation, come up with a single message ("We need to cut costs," or "We should go ahead with project X"). More than one point dilutes the power of your talk.

A common, simple formula, AIDA for short, will help you organize a presentation:

Win their Attention. Start, for instance, with a good story.

Gain their Interest. Show the audience why your topic matters.

Create a Desire. Explain why adopting your view will benefit them.

Elicit Action or Agreement. Spell out what you want from the audience, reinforcing the benefits they'll receive.

This speaking formula is a great way to sell—and that's what you're doing whenever you speak in front of a group.

Well-organized, effective managers acquire skills in presenting and public speaking, and then use them. If you don't have such skills, get a good book on the subject. Better yet, join your local chapter of Toastmasters. It's a godsend—especially for those who would rather face a root canal operation than an audience.

Best Tip
When doing a presentation or speech—or a memo—start with your conclusion. Then offer reasons or arguments that support it.

Written Communications

Electronic media has created another easy way to broadcast to many: e-mail. What once took many phone calls or a memo distributed by hand, taking time and energy, now takes the push of a button.

Alas, e-mail is so useful that people abuse it. Some Silicon Valley managers report receiving upwards of 300 e-mail messages a day. Does the time it takes to go through such a load of mail improve any company's ability to operate? It's doubtful.

Worse, people spend less time composing good messages. It's too easy to sit and type. The result is flaccid, airy prose—often filled with typographical errors—that distorts or confuses the message. That wastes the readers' time, who may have to e-mail you back for clarification.

|Best Tip

Use e-mail sparingly. If you wouldn't call someone or write a paper memo, then don't send e-mail.

Use e-mail, but sparingly. Be especially careful about whom you include on your distribution list for any message. If the message were in paper form, would you send it to so many people? Probably not.

Nothing beats a good paper memo for impact. Save them for important things, and keep the list of those receiving it to the bare minimum. And make sure it's well organized and to the point. There's no surer way to see fuzzy thinking in action than in a memo.

When in doubt, follow the Procter & Gamble model for writing a memo. Keep it to one page, and begin with the words, "This memo . . ." In that line, explain what it's about and what your conclusion is. "This memo will show that we need to improve our guarantee immediately."

Another tip from a pro: "Bottom line on top." State your conclusion first, then give supporting reasons. Don't make people wade through your words to find the nugget at the end. In outline form:

- *Conclusion*
- *Reason*
- *Reason*
- *Reason*
- *Restate conclusion*

In any written communication, use clear, simple, short sentences using concrete words.

Like presenting, writing improves your organizational and communication skills. It forces you to order your thoughts and come to concrete conclusions. It forces you to deal head-on with unclear thinking.

A good memo, electronic or paper, saves you time: It conveys, in the most economical terms, your point. Clear communication, you'll find, greases the organizational wheels like nothing else.

Writing well takes skill. For the ambitious, it's a skill worth cultivating.

Develop a Personal Web Page

Why not put information about you and what you're working on in a personal Web page on the Internet or in a company intranet? Presently, most personal Web pages are vanity items that contain little useful information. But think of the things you could do to save the time it takes to answer questions about your work:

- A work schedule your people or others inside the company or without could consult;
- Frequently requested information;

Best Tip

You'll save hours by posting, on a computer network, the information people now often ask you for.

- Status of projects in process;
- General PR stuff—awards won, quality levels reached, etc.— that make you and your department look good;
- Reports or memos you now distribute by hand or e-mail. (No more filling up e-mail boxes with huge files or spending company time to copy and distribute them.)

In short, post any kind of information that people now bug you or your secretary for on a regular basis, or information that could fend off questions.

For that matter, if you're in a position to post company information—vacation rules, educational reimbursement policies, company holidays, corporate strategies and values—do it. It'll save somebody time.

A Luddite Alternative to E-mail

Good communication systems occur off-line, of course, and one of the best is that perfected by William G. Pagonis.

First a word about Pagonis. A former three-star general in the U.S. Army, he headed the logistics operation in the Gulf War. Some think Pagonis's operation had as much to do with the victory as the tons of bombs dropped on the Iraqis.

Sears, Roebuck snapped up Pagonis upon his retirement to head its logistics. Some laughed at the appointment, doubting he could transfer military-specific skills to the retailer, but Pagonis has contributed in a major way to Sears's resurgence. No one is laughing any more.

Throughout his career, Pagonis has used 3x5-inch index cards to communicate. He writes down a question and routes it to a recipient. The recipient writes an answer and sends it back.

*B*est *T*ip
The lowly index card can be as effective as e-mail—and maybe more so.

Pagonis uses the system to highlight problems, ask questions, and distribute information. He considers it utterly reliable and foolproof.

And he likes it better than e-mail. Why? Because the cards are portable, they and the messages they contain are less ephemeral than e-mail, and, most important, they eliminate lengthy essays. Users must come to the point, and quickly.

Last, there is, in Pagonis's own words, "An implied commitment in one's handwriting . . . that's not there as a result of keyboard pecking."

Does this method speak to you? If so, give it a try. It helped win a war, after all. (And while you're at it, read Pagonis's memoir, *Moving Mountains*.)

The Agile Manager's Checklist

✔ Learn to communicate well. It's a time-management issue.

✔ Save time by speaking to groups.

✔ Use e-mail sparingly.

✔ Learn to write a succinct, well-constructed paper memo. Nothing beats it for impact.

✔ Set up a personal or departmental Web page to distribute reports and memos, and to answer frequently asked questions.

✔ Consider using nontechnical methods to communicate (like a system that uses index cards). They can still offer advantages over computers and telephones.

Chapter Eleven

Use 'Personal Agents'

The Agile Manager sat down late Thursday afternoon with the weekly compilation of articles that his assistant Steve had produced. He silently thanked Steve as he riffled through the folder. There were articles and reviews on:

- A new German manufacturing machine for molded plastic products;
- A software program that guided you through projects;
- A new book that promised to increase your direct-marketing response rates by 20 percent;
- Ways equity participation can motivate employees;
- "Reengineering" new-product development;
- Old-fashioned model trains (an obsession of the Agile Manager);
- The real story behind repetitive-motion syndrome;
- How a noted Japanese inventor comes up with new ideas.

Each of these articles was directly relevant to the Agile Manager's job and interests, and all came from the leading business publications and trade journals. He couldn't count the times the information in these weekly compilations had given him useful ideas and, *once or twice, saved his neck. And saved him time? No question. As he mused, he walked out into the dark outer office and grabbed the latest copy of* Forbes *from the bookshelf behind Steve's desk. He feared that his human filtering system—Steve—would keep him too insulated from news in other fields. As a precaution he occasionally scanned an issue of a magazine from cover to cover.*

I've trained Steve well, thought the Agile Manager. He knows me like a book. But he'll be gone one day. Then what'll I do? He sat down again.

Train someone else to read for me, he thought with a grin.

One key to leveraging yourself—and getting results—is getting others to filter information for you. It's the only way to keep from drowning in the flood of information our society produces.

Sometimes this filter is a person, but having a personal reader is a luxury available to few. Fortunately, whole companies are organized to filter for you.

Use Firms that Filter

Journals, newsletters. Often overlooked as a filtering agent is a good trade journal. If it's doing its job, it will be combing voluminous information sources for items of direct interest to its readers. If it can't find such information, it creates it. Best, most are free to those in the industry the magazine covers. *Industry Week* (1-800-326-4146), for instance, is indispensable for manufacturers. (And anyone in business.)

Best Tip

A good newsletter that tracks your industry or niche is worth its weight in gold—even at $500 a pop.

Just as worthwhile are good newsletters. Though pricey—they often cost $100 or more—they pride themselves on delivering inside information, either by mining public sources or sending reporters to mine the minds of industry experts.

Whatever your field, there's a newsletter for you. Your local library probably has a copy of *The Directory of Newsletters*. Scan it for titles that interest you.

Summary/Abstract/News services. There are three or four companies in the U.S. that specialize in summarizing the best of the year's business books either in print or on tape. They go through the thousands of books published each year, choose the best for you, and present the ideas in concentrated form. The service is worth every penny. The best of these outfits is Soundview Executive Book Summaries. You can reach it at 1-888-358-1000.

Other companies abstract articles on a variety of topics. The reference librarian in your local library can show you where to find them. Reading abstracts can keep you up to date in your field in a relatively painless manner. And you can always choose to read the whole article being abstracted if you want more.

Best Tip

Newstrack—1-888-639-7872—combs business and news publications for articles of interest to senior executives. It puts the full text on tape.

Newstrack (1-888-639-7872) performs a useful service for those who like to listen to their news: Twice monthly, it sends an audio-tape with the full text of articles from *The Economist, Wall Street Journal, Newsweek*, and a host of other magazines. These articles are chosen with the senior executive in mind, so they tend to be on the economy, strategy, and other issues of interest to the CEO.

Personal News/Information Gatherers on the Web

Once you get your computer (and a high-speed modem), take it for a spin on the World Wide Web. Stop in at Newsedge *(www.newsedge.com)*. This firm specializes in hunting and gathering exactly the kind of information you need. And it delivers it to your doorstep—er, fax machine or e-mail box—daily.

Newsedge's premium services will cost you. Others provide modest services for free. One such enterprise is CraYON (*crayon.net*)—Create Your Own Newspaper. CraYON will help you set up a template that draws in, whenever you access it, news of interest to you. It's set up to provide the usual newspaper fare—sports, cartoons, editorials, etc. It assembles the "paper" from public web sites, so don't go looking for that juicy piece of insider information that Newsedge might provide.

Infogate (*www.infogate.com*) also assembles information for you according to your specifications. (It's free, although it delivers ads along with the news.) You download it daily and it feeds news to you over the course of the day as the computer's screensaver.

$Best$ Tip
CraYON (*http://crayon.net*) provides a daily, custom newspaper based on your interests. And it's free.

You need a good computer and high-speed Internet connection to join in the fun. Get wired now; it's worth the expense.

Too Much Information?

All the services mentioned here suggest a paradox: All work to reduce the impact of information overload. Yet all are, themselves, information sources that add to the information that comes into your life. It's possible to go overboard on "personal agents" and feel even more inundated by information.

It's up to you to use discipline. Decide what you want in your life and what you don't. Sternly resist adding things that don't fit your criteria.

My own criterion is simple: If it's merely fun or interesting, whether books, software, magazines, newsletters, or videos, I don't invite more of it into my life. Sadly, for those who make such things, "interesting" and "fun" can be found just about anywhere now, and they are often free.

If something is really useful, however, I want more of it and will pay for it. "Really useful" includes things that help me work smarter or faster, knowledge I can put to use profitably on the job or in maintaining my household, and information that satiates my desire to stay on top of certain subjects.

Let Others Choose for You

It used to be that well-rounded, educated people prided themselves on knowing a little about a lot of things.

I don't have time for that. If I can rely on someone to make a decision in a noncritical area for me, I do. Even if it costs a bit more.

For instance, I'm happy to let a good clothes salesman tell me what shade of blue to wear. I'm happy to let a wine merchant pick the perfect Merlot. If a trusted bookseller thinks I'd like a book in an area I'm browsing, I give it a shot.

Obviously, you have to trust the salesperson or store. And you have to know your basic likes and dislikes. (But who doesn't?)

Our society is filled with experts, even in the most narrow niches. Let the experts be experts. Take their advice. It'll save you hours of having to research questions yourself.

> **Best Tip**
>
> Having the discipline to keep paper and other media at bay is the only known antidote to information overload.

Hold the line, however, in certain areas. We should all have at least one or two subjects in which we know a lot, whether it's rare books, skiing equipment, wine, sailboats, or what have you. Being expert in something is good for your self-esteem.

And be an expert where your business and career are concerned. That's your ultimate job security and from whence your income flows.

The Agile Manager's Checklist

✔ Get others to filter information and news for you. Your best bet: a good trade journal or industry-specific newsletter.

✔ Use computer programs to remember for you, keep you organized, and provide expert solutions.

✔ Use your computer to gather news and analysis on subjects of interest to you.

✔ Let the experts choose for you in areas in which you are unsure of yourself. But always have one or two areas in which you are the expert.

Index